Published by Ice House Books

Planet Cat ® www.PlanetCatStudio.com

Copyright © 2019 Angie Rozelaar courtesy of Yellow House Art Licensing.

Illustrated by Angie Rozelaar

Compiled by Zulekha Afzal & Designed by Richard Peck

Ice House Books is an imprint of Half Moon Bay Limited
The Ice House, 124 Walcot Street, Bath, BA1 5BG
www.icehousebooks.co.uk

ISBN 978-1-912867-15-8

Printed in China

CAT WISDOM

ICE HOUSE BOOKS

"I HAVE LiVED WITH SEVERAL ZEN MASTERS — ALL OF THEM CATS."

- ECKHART TOLLE

"A CAT IS ONLY TECHNICALLY AN ANIMAL, BEING DIVINE."
- ROBERT WILSON LYND

"IN ANCIENT TiMES CATS
WERE WORSHIPPED AS GODS;
THEY HAVE NOT FORGOTTEN THIS."
- TERRY PRATCHETT

"CATS ARE THE WILDEST OF THE TAME AND THE TAMEST OF THE WILD."

– MARK TWAIN

"CATS ARE A MYSTERIOUS KIND OF FOLK.
THERE IS MORE PASSING IN THEIR MINDS
THAN WE ARE AWARE OF."

- SIR WALTER SCOTT

"I LOVE THEM, THEY ARE SO NICE AND SELFISH.
DOGS ARE TOO GOOD AND UNSELFISH.
THEY MAKE ME FEEL UNCOMFORTABLE.
BUT CATS ARE GLORIOUSLY HUMAN."

- L. M. MONTGOMERY

THE CAT OF CATS

I am the cat of cats. I am
The everlasting cat!
Cunning, and old, and sleek as jam,
The everlasting cat!
I hunt vermin in the night –
The everlasting cat!
For I see best without the light –
The everlasting cat!

- WILLIAM BRIGHTY RANDS

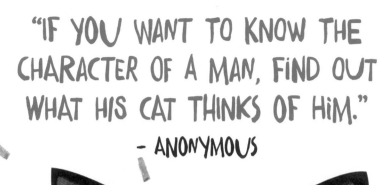

"IF YOU WANT TO KNOW THE CHARACTER OF A MAN, FIND OUT WHAT HIS CAT THINKS OF HIM."

- ANONYMOUS

"I AM AS VIGILANT AS A CAT
TO STEAL CREAM."
- WILLIAM SHAKESPEARE

"THE CAT IS DOMESTIC ONLY AS FAR AS SUITS ITS OWN ENDS."

- SAKI (H. H. MUNRO)

"THE TROUBLE WiTH CATS IS
THAT THEY'VE GOT NO TACT."
– P. G. WODEHOUSE

"THE iDEAL OF CALM
EXISTS IN A SITTING CAT."
- JULES RENARD

ALICE IN WONDERLAND

She was a little startled by seeing the cheshire cat sitting on a bough of a tree a few yards off. The cat only grinned when it saw Alice. It looked good-natured, she thought: still it had *very* long claws and a great many teeth, so she felt it ought to be treated with respect.

"Cheshire puss," she began, rather timidly, as she did not at all know whether it would like the name: however, it only grinned a little wider. "Come, it's pleased so far," thought Alice, and she went on, "Would you tell me, please, which way I ought to walk from here?"

"That depends a good deal on where you want to get to," said the cat.

"I don't much care where—" said Alice.

"Then it doesn't matter which way you walk," said the cat.

"—so long as I get *somewhere*," Alice added as an explanation.

"Oh, you're sure to do that," said the cat, "if you only walk long enough."

- LEWIS CARROLL

"THERE IS NO SNOOZE BUTTON ON A CAT WHO WANTS BREAKFAST."

- ANONYMOUS

"A CAT IS NOBODY'S FOOL."
- HEYWOOD BROUN

"I HAVE STUDIED MANY PHILOSOPHERS AND MANY CATS. THE WISDOM OF CATS IS INFINITELY SUPERIOR."

- HIPPOLYTE A. TAINE

"IT'S REALLY THE CAT'S HOUSE –
WE JUST PAY THE MORTGAGE."
– ANONYMOUS

"IT'S VERY HARD TO BE POLITE IF YOU'RE A CAT."

– ANONYMOUS

THE CAT AND THE MOON

The cat went here and there
And the moon spun round like a top,
And the nearest kin of the moon
The creeping cat looked up.
Black Minnaloushe stared at the moon,
For wander and wail as he would
The pure cold light in the sky
Troubled his animal blood.
Minnaloushe runs in the grass,
Lifting his delicate feet.
Do you dance, Minnaloushe, do you dance?
When two close kindred meet
What better than call a dance?
Maybe the moon may learn,

Tired of that courtly fashion,
A new dance turn.
Minnaloushe creeps through the grass
From moonlit place to place,
The sacred moon overhead
Has taken a new phase.
Does Minnaloushe know that his pupils
Will pass from change to change,
And that from round to crescent,
From crescent to round they range?
Minnaloushe creeps through the grass
Alone, important and wise,
And lifts to the changing moon
His changing eyes.

— WILLIAM BUTLER YEATS

"I PURR, THEREFORE I AM."
- ANONYMOUS

"YOU CAN'T OWN A CAT. THE BEST YOU CAN DO IS BE PARTNERS."

— SIR HARRY SWANSON

"THE LAST THING I WOULD ACCUSE
A CAT OF IS INNOCENCE."
- EDWARD PALEY

"MY HUSBAND SAID IT WAS HIM OR THE CAT . . . I MISS HIM SOMETIMES."
– ZSA ZSA GABOR

THE OWL AND THE PUSSY-CAT

The Owl and the Pussy-cat went to sea
In a beautiful pea green boat,
They took some honey, and plenty of money,
Wrapped up in a five pound note.
The Owl looked up to the stars above,
And sang to a small guitar,
'O lovely Pussy! O Pussy my love,
What a beautiful Pussy you are,
You are,
You are!
What a beautiful Pussy you are!'

Pussy said to the Owl, 'You elegant fowl!
How charmingly sweet you sing!
O let us be married! too long we have tarried:
But what shall we do for a ring?'
They sailed away, for a year and a day,
To the land where the Bong-tree grows
And there in a wood a Piggy-wig stood
With a ring at the end of his nose,
His nose,
His nose,
With a ring at the end of his nose.

'Dear pig, are you willing to sell for one shilling
Your ring?' Said the Piggy, 'I will.'
So they took it away, and were married next day
By the Turkey who lives on the hill.
They dined on mince, and slices of quince,
Which they ate with a runcible spoon;
And hand in hand, on the edge of the sand,
They danced by the light of the moon,
The moon,
The moon,

They danced by the light of the moon.

– EDWARD LEAR

"ALL CATS LIKE BEING THE FOCUS OF ATTENTION."

- PETER GRAY

"THERE ARE NO ORDINARY CATS."

- COLETTE

"A CAT CARES FOR YOU ONLY AS A SOURCE OF FOOD, SECURITY, AND A PLACE IN THE SUN. HER HIGH SELF-SUFFICIENCY IS HER CHARM."

- CHARLES HORTON COOLEY

"IT IS IN THE NATURE OF CATS TO DO A CERTAIN AMOUNT OF UNESCORTED ROAMING."

— ADLAI STEVENSON

"A CAT SLEEPS FAT,
YET WALKS THIN."
- FRED SCHWAB

"THE CAT WAS CREATED WHEN THE LION SNEEZED."

– AL-DAMIRI

"THE DOG MAY BE WONDERFUL PROSE,
BUT ONLY THE CAT IS POETRY."
- FRENCH PROVERB

"CATS ONLY PRETEND TO BE DOMESTICATED IF THEY THINK THERE'S A BOWL OF MILK IN IT FOR THEM."

- ROBIN WILLIAMS

"BY ASSOCIATING WITH THE CAT, ONE ONLY RISKS BECOMING RICHER."

– COLETTE

"A CAT HAS ABSOLUTE EMOTIONAL HONESTY: HUMAN BEINGS, FOR ONE REASON OR ANOTHER, MAY HIDE THEIR FEELINGS, BUT A CAT DOES NOT."

- ERNEST HEMINGWAY

"THE SMALLEST FELINE
IS A MASTERPIECE."
- LEONARDO DA VINCI

"CURIOSITY KILLED THE CAT."
- BEN JONSON

MILK FOR THE CAT

When the tea is brought at five o'clock,
And all the neat curtains are drawn with care,
The little black cat with bright green eyes
Is suddenly purring there.

At first she pretends, having nothing to do,
She has come in merely to blink by the grate,
But, though tea may be late or the milk may be sour,
She is never late.

And presently her agate eyes
Take a soft large milky haze,
And her independent casual glance
Becomes a stiff, hard gaze.

Then she stamps her claws or lifts her ears,
Or twists her tail and begins to stir,
Till suddenly all her lithe body becomes
One breathing, trembling purr.

The children eat and wriggle and laugh,
The two old ladies stroke their silk:
But the cat is grown small and thin with desire,
Transformed to a creeping lust for milk.

The white saucer like some full moon descends
At last from the clouds of the table above;
She sighs and dreams and thrills and glows,
Transfigured with love.

She nestles over the shining rim,
Buries her chin in the creamy sea;
Her tail hangs loose; each drowsy paw
Is doubled under each bending knee.

A long, dim ecstasy holds her life;
Her world is an infinite shapeless white,
Till her tongue has curled the last holy drop,
Then she sinks back into the night,

Draws and dips her body to heap
Her sleepy nerves in the great arm-chair,
Lies defeated and buried deep
Three or four hours unconscious there.

– HAROLD EDWARD MONRO

"I BELIEVE CATS TO BE SPIRITS COME TO EARTH. A CAT, I AM SURE, COULD WALK ON A CLOUD WITHOUT COMING THROUGH."

- JULES VERNE

"IT IS IN THEIR EYES THAT THEIR MAGIC RESIDES."
— ARTHUR SYMONS

"GOD MADE THE CAT IN ORDER TO GIVE MAN THE PLEASURE OF CARESSING THE TIGER."

- ANONYMOUS

"TIME SPENT WITH CATS
IS NEVER WASTED."
– SIGMUND FREUD

"WHAT GREATER GIFT THAN
THE LOVE OF A CAT."

- CHARLES DICKENS